## DATE DUE

|  |  |  |  |
|--|--|--|--|
|  |  |  |  |
|  |  |  |  |
|  |  |  |  |
|  |  |  |  |
|  |  |  |  |
|  |  |  |  |
|  |  |  |  |
|  |  |  |  |
|  |  |  |  |
|  |  |  |  |
|  |  |  |  |
|  |  |  |  |

# LOOKING
## AT SPACE

### DAVID GLOVER

**STAMPLEY**

# How to use this book

### Cross-references
Above some of the chapter titles, you will find a list of other chapters in the book that are related to the topic. Turn to these pages to find out more about each subject.

### See for yourself
See-for-yourself bubbles give you the chance to test out some of the ideas in this book. They explain what you will need and what you have to do to see if an idea really works.

### Quiz corner
In the quiz corner, you will find a list of questions. The answers to the quiz questions are somewhere in the same chapter. Try to answer all the questions about each subject.

### Chatterboxes
Chatterboxes give you interesting facts about other things that are related to the subject.

### Glossary
Difficult words are explained in the glossary on page 31. These words are in **bold** type in the book. Look them up in the glossary to find out what they mean.

### Index
The index is on page 32. It is a list of important words mentioned in the book, with page numbers next to the entries. If you want to read about a subject, look it up in the index, then turn to the page number given.

# Contents

| | | |
|---|---|---|
| What Is Space? | 4 | |
| The Solar System | 6 | |
| Sun and Moon | 8 | |
| Rocky Planets | 10 | |
| Gas Planets | 12 | |
| Stars and Galaxies | 14 | |
| Constellations | 16 | |
| Being an Astronaut | 18 | |

| | |
|---|---|
| Rockets | 20 |
| Space Shuttles | 22 |
| Space Stations | 24 |
| Reaching the Planets | 26 |
| Space Science | 28 |
| Amazing Facts | 30 |
| Glossary | 31 |
| Index | 32 |

# What Is Space?

When you look up at the stars on a clear night, you are looking out into space. Stars, planets, **moons**, **comets**, and **asteroids** are all part of space. All of space and everything in it, including Earth, is called the universe.

### Our planet
We live on a planet called Earth, which is a ball of rock and metal moving through space. Earth seems big to us, but compared with the universe it is tiny.

### Learning about space
Scientists called astronomers study the stars and planets. They use powerful **telescopes** to look out at space. To see even farther into space, rockets launch spacecraft to visit other planets. These spacecraft send closeup pictures of the planets and their moons back to Earth.

◀ People who travel into space are called astronauts. They wear special suits to protect their bodies and to help them breathe.

### Bright stars
There are millions of stars in space. Stars look like tiny pinpoints of light, but really they are huge balls of burning gas. Our Sun is a star. It looks brighter than all the other stars because it is closer to Earth.

**WARNING:**
**Never look straight at the Sun with or without binoculars. It is so bright that it can damage your eyes.**

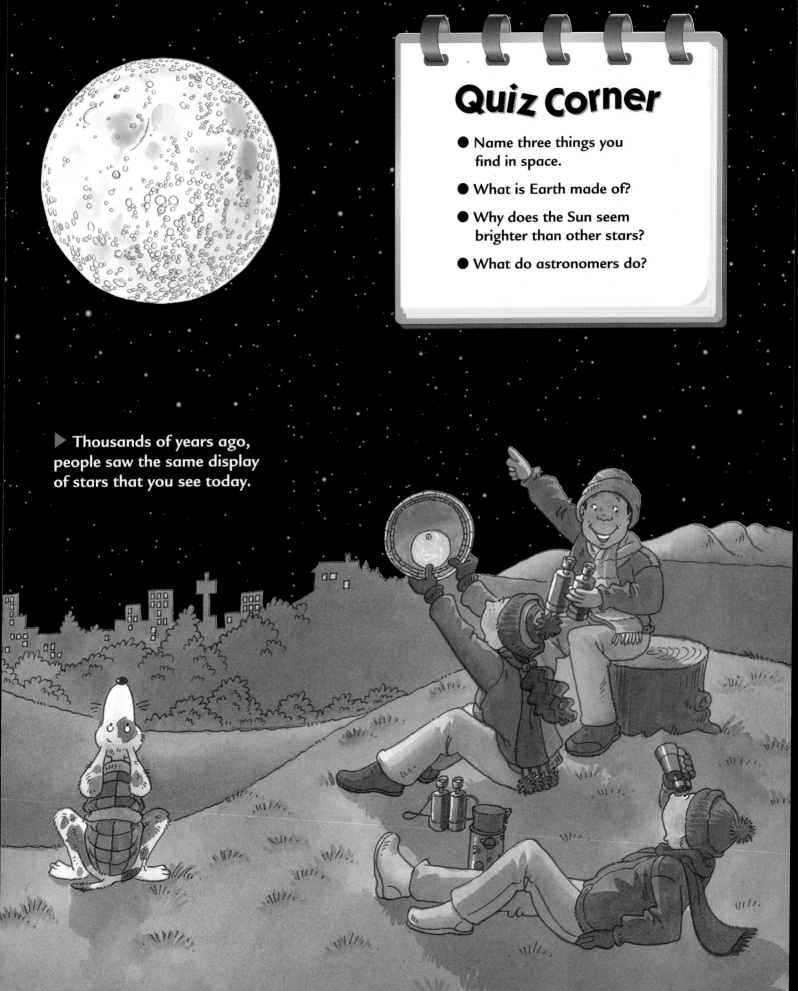

## Quiz Corner

- Name three things you find in space.

- What is Earth made of?

- Why does the Sun seem brighter than other stars?

- What do astronomers do?

▶ Thousands of years ago, people saw the same display of stars that you see today.

# The Solar System

A solar system is the name we give to a sun and all the things that go around, or **orbit,** it. Our solar system includes nine planets and more than 60 **moons.** Many smaller objects that orbit the Sun, such as **comets** and **asteroids,** are also part of the solar system.

## The planets

The nine planets of our solar system are different sizes and are at different distances from the Sun. Mercury is the closest, then Venus, Earth, Mars, Jupiter, Saturn, Uranus, Neptune, and Pluto. They all orbit at different speeds. It takes one year for Earth to go around the Sun one time.

### Gravity and orbits

On Earth, a force called **gravity** pulls all objects toward the planet's surface. Larger objects in space, such as the Sun, have a stronger pull of gravity. The Sun's gravity keeps the planets in their orbits and stops them from drifting away.

Pluto......

Jupiter

Sun

Mars

Venus

.....Uranus

...Earth

Mercury

Saturn

Neptune

▶ This illustration shows the sizes of the planets compared with each other. The comparative distances between the planets are much greater than shown here.

*Pluto is the smallest planet, even smaller than our moon.*

*Neptune is a blue planet, covered in places by wispy white clouds.*

*Uranus spins at a different slant than the other planets.*

*Saturn has many colorful rings around its middle.*

6

All the planets except for Earth are named after Greek or Roman gods. Venus was the Roman goddess of love, Neptune was the Roman god of the sea, and Uranus was the Greek god of the sky.

Mercury is only slightly bigger than our moon.

Venus is wrapped in thick, poisonous clouds.

Earth's surface is mostly covered with water.

The Sun is at the center of the solar system.

Mars looks red when seen from Earth.

**Asteroids and comets**
Asteroids are lumps of rock in space. Millions of asteroids orbit the Sun between Mars and Jupiter. Comets are balls of snow and dust that follow an oval-shaped orbit, rather than a circular orbit, around the Sun. When a comet is close to the Sun, the snow turns to gas and makes a long tail.

Jupiter is the largest planet and, after Venus, is the easiest planet to spot in the night sky.

# Quiz Corner

- Which is the smallest planet?
- What is at the center of the solar system?
- How long does Earth take to orbit the Sun?
- What is a comet's tail made of?

Look at: Stars and Galaxies, page 14; Rockets, page 20

# Sun and Moon

The Sun is millions of miles away from Earth. Even from this distance, its heat and light warm our planet and make plants grow. The Sun is four hundred times larger than the Moon. The Moon is a cold ball of rock that moves around Earth. It is one-fourth as large as Earth. There is no air, no water, and no life on the Moon.

### Days and nights
While Earth **orbits** the Sun, it spins—once every 24 hours. We call this length of time one day. When the side of Earth where you live faces the Sun, it is daytime. When it is turned away from the Sun, it is nighttime.

············ *daytime*

··········· *nighttime*

▲ As Earth spins from day into night, the Sun starts to disappear from view.

▶ In the same way that Earth orbits the Sun, the Moon orbits Earth.

**The changing Moon**
The Moon looks bright in the night sky, but it does not give out its own light. It shines because, like a mirror, it **reflects** light from the Sun. Each night, the Moon appears to be a slightly different shape. This is because our view of the sunlit side of the Moon changes as the Moon orbits Earth.

*Earth* ............

▼ Every month, the Moon takes about two weeks to go from new to full. It takes another two weeks to become new again.

*The Moon takes about one month to orbit Earth once.*

*new moon*

*crescent moon*

*first quarter*

*full moon*

## SEE FOR YOURSELF

*The Moon is covered with huge hollows called **craters**. These are made when objects crash into the Moon's surface. Fill a bowl with flour and drop in some pebbles. Lift the pebbles out and discover your own Moon surface.*

# Quiz Corner

● How long does it take Earth to make one full spin?

● How long does it take the Moon to orbit Earth?

● Which is larger, the Sun or the Moon?

Look at: The Solar System, page 6; Reaching the Planets, page 26

# Rocky Planets

The four planets closest to the Sun—Mercury, Venus, Earth, and Mars—are called rocky planets. They are balls of rock with metal cores. Pluto, the farthest planet from the Sun, is also a rocky planet. It is thought to be made entirely of rock.

▼ Mercury has many mountains and **craters**. It looks similar to the Moon, but it is much hotter.

**CHATTERBOX**

Some scientists believe that there may have been life on Mars millions of years ago, when there was flowing water on the planet. However, the *Viking* space probes that landed on Mars in 1976 found no signs of life, nor did the *Pathfinder* probe which landed on Mars in 1997.

▶ The hot surface of Venus is covered with rocky mountains and wide craters. Thick clouds make the sky orange.

## Inside Earth

Earth's surface is called the crust. Below the crust, there is a layer of rock called the mantle. Below this, there is a layer of hot liquid metal called the outer core. Earth's center, or inner core, is solid metal.

............ crust

.... mantle

... outer core

...... inner core

## Mercury and Venus

As one part of Mercury turns to face the Sun, the **temperature** becomes hot enough to melt lead. At night, as that part of the planet turns away from the Sun, the land becomes freezing. Venus is farther away from the Sun than Mercury, but its surface is hotter. The layer of gas that surrounds Venus traps heat.

## Earth and Mars

Earth is at just the right distance from the Sun for life to exist. It is neither too hot nor too cold. As far as we know, it is the only planet that has flowing water. Mars is smaller than Earth and much colder. There is water on Mars, but it is frozen at the top and bottom of the planet.

## Pluto

Pluto was discovered in 1930. It has one **moon**, which is almost as big as Pluto itself. Pluto is still a mystery to astronomers. So far, it has not been explored by any spacecraft.

## Quiz Corner

- What are the names of the rocky planets?
- Has life been discovered anywhere other than on Earth?
- What is at the center of Earth?
- How many moons does Pluto have?

Look at: The Solar System, page 6; Reaching the Planets, page 26

# Gas Planets

Jupiter, Saturn, Uranus, and Neptune are often called the gas giants. They are large planets made of gas and liquids. All of the gas planets have rings made up of pieces of rock. Astronauts have not visited these planets. The planets are too far away and do not have a hard surface on which to land.

▶ Saturn has the most spectacular rings of all the gas planets.

*As Saturn spins,* ...................................... *winds blow the gases around the planet into stripes.*

▼ Jupiter is a bright orange planet with one narrow ring.

*Great Red Spot*

## Jupiter and Saturn

Jupiter is the largest planet in the solar system. It is 11 times bigger than Earth. Jupiter spins faster than the other planets, and fierce storms rage on its surface. One of these, called the Great Red Spot, has lasted for over 300 years. Saturn is the second largest planet and has at least 22 **moons**. Three of its bright rings can be seen from Earth with a **telescope**.

▼ Uranus is surrounded by a thick blue layer of gas.

▼ Neptune is slightly smaller than Uranus. It is the farthest gas giant from the Sun.

*Saturn's rings were the first rings to be discovered ............. around a planet.*

**CHATTERBOX**

Nearly 400 years ago, the Italian astronomer Galileo pointed one of the first telescopes toward Jupiter. He discovered 4 of Jupiter's 16 moons. Galileo was the first person to see moons around a planet other than Earth.

*Anne's Spot, discovered in 1980, is a ............................... giant storm.*

**Uranus and Neptune**

Uranus has at least 15 moons. It is the only gas planet on which astronomers have not found clouds or storms. On Neptune, winds blow at over three times the speed of the strongest winds on Earth. Triton, Neptune's largest moon, is the coldest place in the solar system.

## Quiz Corner

- Which is the largest planet in the solar system?
- How many moons does Saturn have?
- Where is the coldest place in the solar system?

Look at: Constellations, page 16

# Stars and Galaxies

Stars are balls of gas that burn for millions of years. Each one belongs to a huge spinning group of stars called a **galaxy**. The Sun and most of the stars we see in the sky are part of a galaxy called the Milky Way. It is one of billions of galaxies in space.

## Big distances

Most stars in the Milky Way are so far away that even if you traveled in an airplane for one million years you would not reach them. Their light takes hundreds of years to reach us. The light from one distant star may take so long to reach us that by the time we see it, the star itself may have died.

▼ Stars are born from huge clouds of gas and dust called nebulae.

**A star is born**
Over millions of years, gas and dust in a **nebula** are pulled into a ball by **gravity**. The ball heats up and glows as a bright star. As the gas runs out, the star begins to die.

*1. A star comes to life.*

*2. After millions of years, the star grows and begins to turn red.*

*3. Some stars die with a bang.*

▼ **Our galaxy, the Milky Way, is shaped like a spiral.**

*The center of the Milky Way is hidden by a fog of stardust.*

*Our solar system is near the edge of the Milky Way.*

**Moving through space**
Some galaxies have spiral arms, others are oval-shaped, and others are uneven. Like all objects in space, galaxies spin. Astronomers have discovered that they are moving away from each other, traveling farther into space.

# Quiz Corner

- What is the name of our galaxy?
- How long do stars live?
- What shape is our galaxy?
- How many galaxies are in space?

Look at: Stars and Galaxies, page 14

# Constellations

When you look at the night sky, the bright stars seem to make patterns. In ancient times, people named these patterns after animals, heroes, and gods. Today, we call these patterns constellations. We use them to make maps of the night sky.

**Spinning around**

Throughout the year, as Earth **orbits** the Sun, the constellations seem to move through the sky. In the Northern Hemisphere, one star appears to stay in the same place. This star is called the North Star because it is always directly above the North Pole. Sailors and other travelers use it to find their way at night.

**Half and half**

Earth is divided into two halves called hemispheres. People who live in the Northern Hemisphere see a different set of stars than people who live in the Southern Hemisphere.

...... *Northern Hemisphere*

...... *Southern Hemisphere*

▼ Here are some constellations that can be seen from parts of the Northern Hemisphere, such as Europe, North America, and China.

Great Bear

North Star

Little Bear

Queen Cassiopeia

King Cepheus

Dragon

16

Buy a simple star map called a planisphere to help you spot constellations in the night sky. Use it to find out which constellations appear at different times of the year.

- What are patterns of stars called?
- What is a planisphere?
- Which constellation includes the North Star?
- Name some constellations in the Southern Hemisphere.

▼ Here are some constellations that can be seen from parts of the Southern Hemisphere, such as Australia and parts of South America.

*The Sail, Keel, and Stern constellations make up a sailing ship.*

Centaur

Scorpion

Sail

Stern

Southern Cross

Keel

Look at: Rockets, page 20; Space Stations, page 24

# Being an Astronaut

Astronauts travel into space to repair equipment, to perform experiments, or simply to explore. In 1961, the Russian Yuri Gagarin became the first person in space when he orbited Earth in the spacecraft *Vostok 1*. Since then, many astronauts have spent weeks or even months living in space.

**CHATTERBOX**

In space, people can move around without much effort. Standing, sitting, and even running are so easy that muscles begin to lose their strength. To stay fit, astronauts work out regularly on special machines.

### Feeling weightless
Far away from Earth, where spacecraft travel, astronauts do not feel **gravity**. Things float in midair unless they are fixed to something else. All equipment inside the spacecraft has to be stored in cupboards or attached to walls.

### Space suits
A space suit protects an astronaut from the chill of space and the heat of the Sun's rays. There is no air to breathe in space, so an astronaut's space suit is filled with **oxygen** for breathing.

▶ To move freely outside the craft, an astronaut can be strapped into a moving chair called a Manned Maneuvering Unit, or MMU.

*The astronaut ........................ steers the MMU using controls on the armrests.*

*A camera sends photographs back to the spacecraft.*

*A visor protects the astronaut's face from the Sun.*

▲ Some of an astronaut's training takes place under water where, as in space, everything feels lighter.

### Astronaut school

It takes years of training to prepare for a journey into space. Astronauts learn how to use equipment that will keep them alive in space. They need to be able to cope with any emergency. They also practice experiments that they will carry out on board their spacecraft.

*The oxygen supply lasts for seven hours.*

*A chest pack carries the computer controls.*

# Quiz Corner

● Who was the first person in space?

● What does an astronaut need to learn before going into space?

● Where do astronauts do some of their training?

Look at: Space Shuttles, page 22

# Rockets

Rocket power is used to launch all kinds of spacecraft, such as **satellites** and **space shuttles**. A rocket needs tremendous power to lift its load away from Earth and into space. **Fuel** burns inside the rocket, making hot gases rush out of the bottom. This jet of fiery heat pushes the rocket upward.

▶ *Ariane 5 is Europe's biggest rocket. It can carry as many as four satellites into space.*

## SEE FOR YOURSELF

*See how a rocket launches into space. Blow up a balloon and then let it go. The blast of air from the balloon pushes it forward. In the same way, hot gases push a rocket up into space.*

### Satellites in space

A satellite is a spacecraft that **orbits** Earth. It has no people on board. Rockets launch all kinds of satellites. Space **telescopes** are satellites that look out into space. They send information about stars and **galaxies** to Earth. Weather satellites take pictures of Earth to help people predict the weather.

## Launching a satellite

*Ariane 5* is made up of two **booster rockets** and two main sections called stages. After takeoff, the booster rockets and first stage fall away.

*second stage*

*first stage*

**booster .... rocket**

**1. When the booster rockets have run out of fuel, they fall away.**

**2. The protective covering comes away.**

**3. The first stage separates and the second stage carries the satellite into space.**

▲ Only 12 people have ever walked on the Moon. The first, Neil Armstrong, planted an American flag.

## First to the Moon

In 1969, a huge American rocket launched a spacecraft called *Apollo 11* toward the Moon. After the rocket stages fell away, *Apollo 11* carried the astronauts close to the Moon. Then the spacecraft sent a lander that carried two astronauts, Neil Armstrong and Buzz Aldrin, down to the Moon's surface. These men became the first people to land on the Moon.

## Quiz Corner

- What do rockets carry into space?
- What is the name of Europe's biggest rocket?
- Who were the first two people to walk on the Moon?

Look at: Rockets, page 20; Space Stations, page 24

# Space Shuttles

A **space shuttle** is a spacecraft that can be used more than once. Shuttles have taken many astronauts to space and back. They also deliver **cargo** to **space stations**, returning with equipment in need of repair or with the results of experiments.

▶ A shuttle is launched by two **booster rockets** and a huge **fuel** tank. These fall away after takeoff.

**The cargo bay**
**Satellites** and other pieces of equipment are stored in a large area in the top of the shuttle called the cargo bay. Satellites can be launched or repaired using a robot arm that reaches out of the cargo bay.

**Life on board**
A trip on the shuttle lasts about nine days. Astronauts breathe the air inside the shuttle and do not need space suits. They sleep in bunks or in bags strapped to the walls. Without the straps, the astronauts would float around.

◀ Before the shuttle lands on Earth, the pilot turns off its engines. It lands like an airplane does, but it needs a longer runway.

▶ In 1990, a space shuttle launched the Hubble Space Telescope, which sends pictures of galaxies to Earth.

## Quiz Corner

- What is kept in the shuttle's cargo bay?
- How is the shuttle's robot arm used?
- Do astronauts need to wear space suits inside the shuttle?
- Where do astronauts sleep?

*This astronaut is using the shuttle's robot arm to help repair part of the Hubble Space Telescope.*

Look at: Being an Astronaut, 18; Space Shuttles, page 22

# Space Stations

A **space station** is a large spacecraft where astronauts live and conduct experiments. In the future, space stations may be used as factories where special materials and medicines will be made. Space stations may also become the starting points for trips to other planets.

### Mir space station

In 1986, the Russians launched a space station called *Mir*. It is made up of different parts, called modules, which were launched by rockets and fitted together in space. There are always astronauts on *Mir*. Some astronauts spend over a year on board before returning to Earth.

▼ Here, the spacecraft *Soyuz* is docking with the main module of *Mir*.

*Spacecraft, such as Soyuz, bring astronauts to* Mir.

*New modules join with* Mir *at the docking port.*

*Astronauts climb through a hatch to enter* Mir *from the docking port.*

## CHATTERBOX

Astronauts on *Mir* have to be careful not to let their food float away while they are eating. It might get into important equipment.

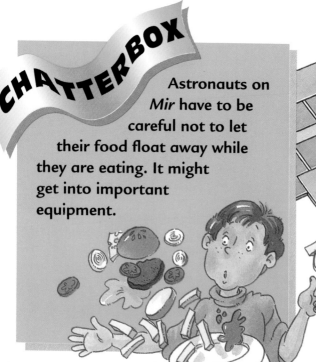

### Extra rooms

Each of *Mir*'s modules is used for different activities. The main module is the living area, while a smaller module is used as a space **observatory**. The MMU, used by astronauts to make repairs outside the station, is stored in a separate module.

▶ *Mir*'s final module was added in 1996. Today, **space shuttles** carry astronauts and equipment to *Mir*.

*Panels on each side of the station use the Sun's rays to make electricity.*

*Inside* Mir, *astronauts do not have to wear space suits.*

*Astronauts eat, sleep, and work in* Mir's *main module.*

**Accidents in space**

In 1997, a delivery craft crashed into the side of *Mir*. Luckily nobody was hurt, but many experiments were lost. In the future, scientists hope to build a larger and safer space station, called *International Space Station*, which may be connected to *Mir*.

# Quiz Corner

- How long have some astronauts stayed on *Mir*?

- Where do *Mir*'s new modules join to the main module?

- How does *Mir* make electricity?

- What happened to *Mir* in 1997?

Look at: Rocky Planets, page 10; Gas Planets, page 12

# Reaching the Planets

Astronauts have traveled only as far as the Moon, but scientists can explore the planets using machines called space probes. These send information and pictures back to scientists on Earth. Space probes have landed on, or flown by, all of the planets in the solar system except for Pluto.

### Voyager 2
The *Voyager 2* probe was launched in 1977. It has flown around Jupiter, Saturn, Uranus, and Neptune, beaming pictures of the planets and their **moons** back to Earth. It is now heading out of the solar system and into outer space.

Saturn

Jupiter

Earth

Uranus

Neptune

▼ Probes have landed on Mars and sent back detailed pictures of its rocky red surface.

### Searching for life
*Voyager 2* carries a special recording called "Sounds of Earth," which is a greeting to any living creature who might find the probe. The recording has words in more than 60 languages and music from countries all over the world.

In 1995, after a six-year journey, the *Galileo* space probe reached Jupiter. It dropped a smaller probe into Jupiter's clouds to study its layers of gas. The small probe sent closeup pictures of the planet back to Earth.

# Quiz Corner

- Which planets has *Voyager 2* visited?
- What does the surface of Mars look like?
- How long did it take *Galileo* to reach Jupiter?

◀ After *Galileo* released the small probe, it **orbited** Jupiter, visiting four of its moons.

Look at: Rockets, page 20

# Space Science

Space exploration is only possible because of the work of scientists. Scientists continue to make new rockets and space probes to help us find out more about the universe. While designing space equipment, they have discovered many new materials that can be useful on Earth as well as in space.

▶ These runners' capes are made of a material first designed for astronauts' clothing.

## Learning from space

We now know much more about how stars and planets are made and about how the universe began. Space science has also changed our everyday lives. Smoke detectors, fireproof clothing, and lightweight materials for safety helmets and tennis shoes are all the result of research into space travel.

### Communication

Some **satellites** are launched into space to help people on Earth communicate with each other. They can bounce telephone or television signals almost instantly from one side of Earth to the other.

*1. A caller speaks into a telephone in the United States.*

*2. The signal bounces off a satellite.*

*3. The signal reaches a person in Africa.*

▼ **One day, astronauts might visit Mars. This is how some scientists imagine Mars might look in the future.**

*People and animals would need to wear space suits.*

*Plants in giant greenhouses would provide some of the food.*

## Quiz Corner

● For what are communication satellites used?

● How many inventions can you name that were a result of space science?

● Which planet might people visit in the future?

People would travel to other parts of Mars in special landers.

Cars would need thick tires to cope with the rough Martian landscape.

People would use satellite dishes to send messages to Earth.

# Amazing Facts

● Some scientists believe that the universe was made 15 billion years ago from a huge explosion called the big bang.

☆ *Radio waves carrying our radio and television programs never disappear. They shoot into space, traveling millions of miles each year. One day, life on distant planets —if there is any—could tune into our shows!*

● The highest mountain in the solar system is Olympus Mons on Mars. It is three times higher than Mount Everest.

☆ *People are taller in space. On Earth, **gravity** holds the bones of our bodies closer together. In space, people don't feel gravity, so the bones of people in space gap.*

● Story Musgrave, an American, is one of the world's most experienced astronauts. In 1996, at 61 years old, he became the oldest astronaut to travel in space.

☆ *Stars are different colors depending on how hot they are. The hottest stars are blue and the next hottest are blue-white or white. Stars that have a medium heat are yellow, and the coolest ones are red.*

● The most distant stars you can see without a **telescope** are in the Andromeda **galaxy**. Light from this galaxy takes more than two million years to reach Earth.

☆ *The first animal in space was a dog named Laika. She flew on the Russian **satellite** Sputnik II in 1957.*

● People used to think that the dark areas on the Moon were seas. We now know that they are huge patches of dark rock.

☆ *Scientists have sent a radio message to a group of stars called M13. The message will take 25,000 years to arrive, so we cannot expect a reply for at least 50,000 years.*

# Glossary

**asteroid** A piece of rock that **orbits** the Sun.

**booster rocket** An engine that gives extra power for liftoff. It falls away seconds after the main rocket has been launched.

**cargo** The equipment, food, and other goods that spacecraft carry.

**comet** A ball of snow and dust that moves around the Sun.

**crater** A hollow in a planet or a **moon**, made by an object crashing into its surface.

**fuel** A material that burns in an engine and makes it work.

**galaxy** An organized group of millions of stars.

**gravity** The force that pulls objects toward the center of the Earth, makes things have weight.

**moon** An object in space that travels around a planet. A moon is smaller than its planet.

**nebula** A cloud of gas and dust in space.

**observatory** A place where astronomers use **telescopes** and other machines to study space.

**orbit** The curved path of an object in space as it travels around a larger object. Earth orbits the Sun, while the Moon orbits Earth.

**oxygen** A gas in the air on Earth. Animals and plants need oxygen to live.

**reflect** To bounce light back. We see the Moon because it reflects light from the Sun.

**satellite** A machine or body in space that **orbits** another body.

**space shuttle** A spacecraft that can be used more than once.

**space station** A spacecraft that **orbits** Earth with people on board. Astronauts may work there for several months.

**telescope** A tube with glass lenses or curved mirrors that makes distant objects look bigger and clearer.

**temperature** How hot or cold something is.

# Index

## A

Aldrin, Buzz **21**
Andromeda galaxy **30**
Anne's Spot **13**
*Apollo 11* **21**
*Ariane 5* **20, 21**
Armstrong, Neil **21**
asteroid **4, 6, 7**
astronaut **4, 12, 18-19, 22, 23, 24, 25, 26, 30**
astronomer **4, 13, 15**

## B

big bang **30**

## C

comet **4, 6, 7**
constellation **16-17**

## E

Earth **4, 6, 7, 8, 9, 10, 11, 16, 28**

## G

Gagarin, Yuri **18**
galaxy **14-15, 20, 23**
Galileo **13**
*Galileo* probe **27**
gravity **15, 18, 30**
Great Red Spot **12**

## H

Hubble Space Telescope **23**

## I

*International Space Station* **25**

## J

Jupiter **6, 7, 12, 13, 26, 27**

## M

M13 **30**
Manned Maneuvering Unit (MMU) **18, 24**
Mars **6, 7, 10, 11, 28**
Mercury **6, 7, 10, 11**
Milky Way **14**
*Mir* **24, 25**
Moon **6, 7, 8-9, 21, 26, 30**
Musgrave, Story **30**

## N

nebula **14, 15**
Neptune **6, 12, 13, 26**
North Star **16**

## O

Olympus Mons **30**

## P

planisphere **17**
Pluto **6, 10, 11, 26**

## R

rocket **4, 20-21, 28**

## S

satellite **20, 22, 24, 28**
Saturn **6, 12, 13, 26**
solar system **6-7, 15, 26**
*Soyuz* **24**
space probe **10, 26, 27, 28**
space shuttle **20, 22-23, 25**
space station **22, 24-25**
space suit **4, 18, 22, 25, 28**
*Sputnik II* **30**
star **4, 14-15, 16, 17, 20, 23, 28, 30**
Sun **4, 6, 7, 8-9, 10, 14, 16, 18, 25**

## T

telescope **4, 12, 13, 20, 23**
Triton **13**

## U

Uranus **6, 12, 13, 26**

## V

Venus **6, 7, 10, 11**
Viking spacecraft **10**
*Vostok 1* **18**
*Voyager 2* **26**

Published in the USA by
C.D. Stampley Enterprises, Inc.,
Charlotte, NC, USA.
Created by Two-Can Publishing Ltd.,
London. English language edition
©Two-Can Publishing Ltd, 1998

Managing Editor: Robert Sved
Art Director: Carole Orbell
Senior Designer: Gareth Dobson
Editor: Janet De Saulles
Picture research: Laura Cartwright
Consultant: Carole Stott
Artwork: Stuart Trotter, Teri Gower,
Mel Pickering, Jason Lewis
Production: Adam Wilde
Additional Research: Inga Phipps

ISBN 1-58087-000-7

Photographic credits: front cover:
Pictor; pp. 4, 8: Planet Earth Pictures;
p. 10: NASA/Science Photo Library;
p. 14: Royal Observatory,
Edinburgh/AAO/Science Photo
Library; p. 19: NASA/Science Photo
Library; p. 22(t): Pictor International;
p. 22(b): NASA/Science Photo
Library; p. 23: Planet Earth Pictures;
pp. 25, 26: NASA; p. 29: PA News.